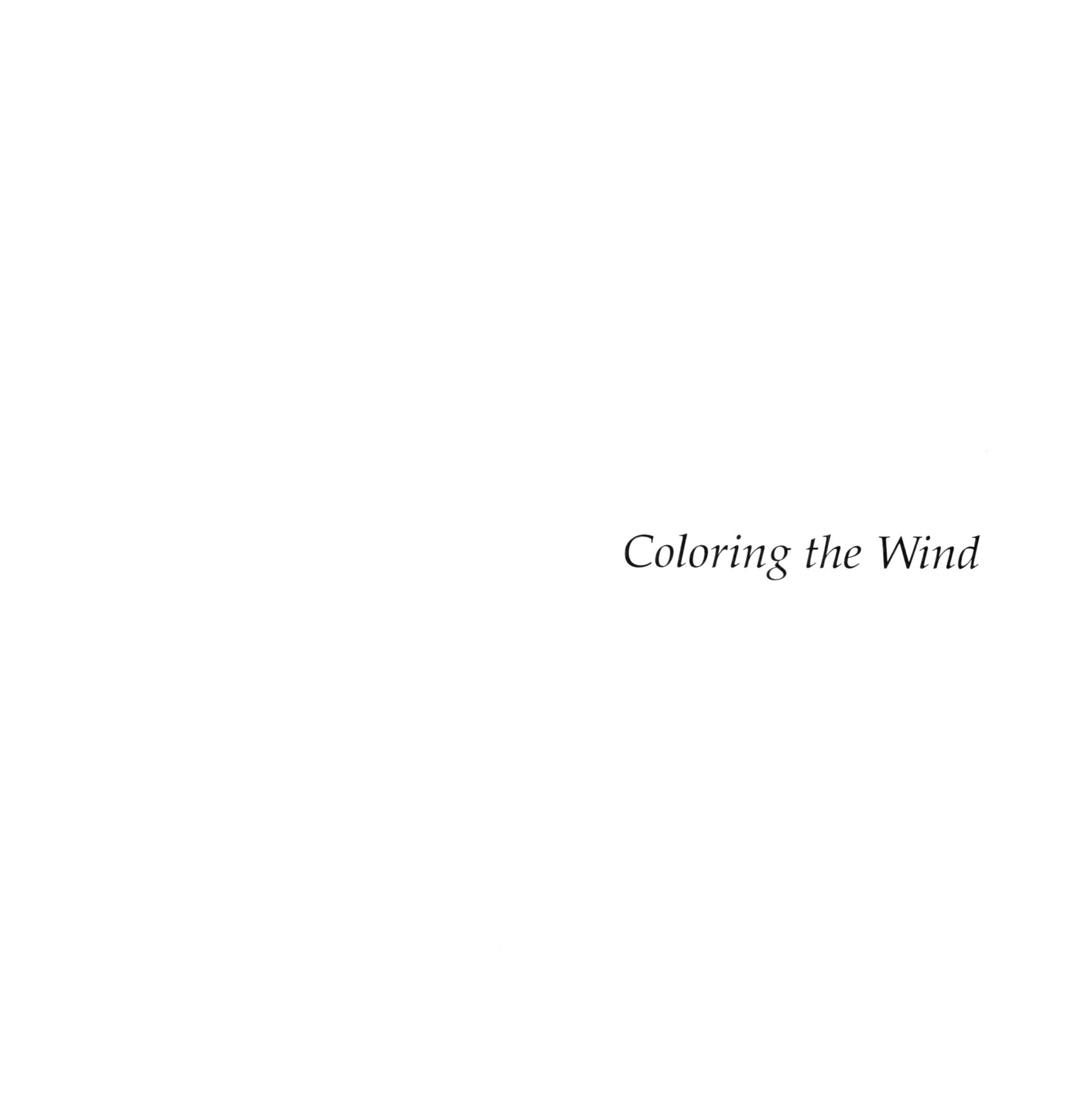

Coloring the Wind

Coloring the Wind

Using
Photos
and
Words

Frances,
May the color
in your wind
be love.
Shalom,
Dave

David P. Young

Westminster/John Knox Press
Louisville, Kentucky

Book design by Denominational Resources

First edition

This book is printed on acid-free paper that meets the American National Standards Institute Z39.48 standard. ♾

Published by Westminster/John Knox Press
Louisville, Kentucky

PRINTED IN MEXICO
9 8 7 6 5 4 3 2 1

Library of Congress Cataloging-in-Publication Data

Young, David P. (David Paris), 1937–
Coloring the wind : using photos and words / David P. Young. —
1st ed.
p. cm.
ISBN 0-664-25376-8

1. Meditations. I. Title.
BV4832.2.Y58 1992
242—dc20 91-45742

Dedication

To those many persons who have looked at me
through my camera and let me paint a moment
of their lives on film, and

To the renewal of hope that continually comes
as witness from those whose poverty comes
at the hands of the powerful who value their power
more than compassion, justice, and love.

As children, we had more abandon than as adults. When we first learned to color we did it with large, winding, slashing, bold strokes. Later we were taught the rules: about lines and not coloring one space with more than one color and what looks nice and what does not.

As adults, living is all too often squeezed into busyness. Too much to do. Run from one thing to another.

Life, though, offers more than busyness, more than rules for coloring. There are other kinds of moments.

This book is an invitation to encounter those other kinds of moments. Through word pictures and photos without words we are invited to experience once again some of the abandon of a child.

Nicaragua

God help me understand
what I must let loose of
in order to have
the freedom to
grasp what you
are holding out

some people
are so busy
they never
create
memories

Peace is the
greatest thing
to fear,

for to get it
would require
the most change.

There are those who see
peace only as protecting
themselves.

And others who see it as
sharing themselves.

God hides
so that those
who have enough
faith will look.

For too many people, as
Far away as they can see
is themselves.

There
must
be
a
thousand
melodies,

a
thousand
and
one
different
ways

that
God
knows
to
bring
the
rain
to
the
earth.

Nicaragua

To Color the Wind

(Living the Best Dream You Can)

The Queen once remarked to Alice in Lewis Carroll's *Through the Looking-Glass* that she had sometimes believed as many as six impossible things before breakfast. What if we took the Queen seriously and did more reflecting and acting on the "impossibles" of peace and justice and taking the environment seriously? What if we shared together the best dreams we have for a better life? What if we decided to color the wind?

To color the wind is a metaphor for thinking about the world with a different passion than usual. A passion that believes good change is possible. A passion that believes, if we have been determined to use military force as a means of being in control, that we can be determined to use cooperation instead. A passion that is serious about the presence of compassion and love. A passion that says we must seek out new relationships with self, with others, with nature, and with God. A passion that is willing to focus on the impossible—not because suddenly it has become possible, but because it is what God requires of us, in faith and action.

To color the wind is also a metaphor for living the best dream we can be. It is paying attention to the colors, to life, and seeking those which are most pleasing in God's sight.

To find the colors and the wind we have to be willing to look into our experiences so we can see again the insanity of our ways and gain the courage to develop new skills for being and living. Without new skills we will continue with knowledge that is used more for exploitation and control than for faithfulness to God's call for justice and love.

Alice told the Queen that there was no use trying. "One *can't* believe impossible things." But why not? Like the tearing down of the Berlin Wall (or Jericho) or a white president in South Africa releasing from twenty-six years in prison a black leader or free elections in communist countries.

Why not color the wind and create new relationships?

Haiti

Hope is the belief
that God will
still surprise.

Hope is the journey,
not the destination.

—truth is what the powerful
 lie about to stay in power

—telling the truth takes
 more nerve than lying

—lies require the habit of
 them to make them look
 like truth

idle thought: on the yellow
brick road there are enough
oil slicks that no one has
visited the wizard in quite
a while

sleeping in church
and banking on God's
willingness to look
the other way

I carry a street corner
  around with me so
I will have a place
  to stand when
I want to watch the
  world go by.

God has set the table.
There are more places
Than people because
Most think you have to
Buy a ticket to get in.

Little boy.
Belly larger than his head.
A stomach trying to learn
how to eat from air.
If that belly was full of food,
he would grow seven feet tall,
grinning at the joy of living.

Candles in a church . . .
patient light waiting
for God to notice.

God I chase you always.
I make you run
The other way.
I throw stones
And sticks at you.

Then I cry in the night,
Where are you?

In my pocket I carry
balloons already blown up.
I like the look of
surprise on people's
faces when I pull
one out.

perhaps we are in a quiet time

not a time for grand ideas
and magnificent schemes
or righteous revolution

but a gestation, like a
bulb resting in winter
ground

spring will come;
will we be ready?

Nicaragua

Two Walls

As I took my first steps on the flagstone walkway alongside the Vietnam Wall in Washington, D.C., my first thoughts were of disappointment: This monument is small. It isn't very big. It isn't very high, and it isn't very long. But as I walked down the sloping walkway and the wall grew taller, I was soon overwhelmed. Engulfed by height, I was made aware of the silence in lives and families created by a war that never made sense, nor does now. The names were looking out at me . . . silences that should still be speaking, living.

By the time I had gotten to the area where the wall was its tallest, higher than I could reach even by jumping, the weight of the fifty thousand names so cleanly chiseled into it became very noticeable. I stopped walking because I could not move against their weight. The impact was heightened by watching a woman standing on a stepladder, reaching still higher over her head to make a pencil rubbing of a name.

A name. Fifty thousand names. Fifty thousand wasted U.S. lives, five hundred thousand wasted Vietnamese lives in a war supposed to be for democracy. It turned out to be for waste, pure waste of human lives. The weight of those five hundred and fifty thousand names is still firmly attached to the soul of the United States.

Later, however, I found a greater power and symbolism to the wall than the weight of those names. It is the power of forgetting. When you leave the wall and walk around behind it along a sidewalk the wall disappears. You are no more than twenty or thirty yards away but you can't see it anymore because the wall is set into the ground. Whoever heard of a monument you can't see?

Yes, the wall can disappear, which is also what we in the United States have tried to do with the war in Vietnam. To forget it. To put it in the history books where it will be safe in the past. But it won't go away because the wall has fifty thousand names. Thus, in reality, there are two walls in that monument: one is the image of how we forget (when seen from behind) and the other the image of how we remember (when we face it).

The surface of the wall is highly reflective, and you can't look at it without also seeing yourself or others. While watching reflections pass on the wall, watching them play over the names of the silent, I overheard a mother answer her child. I did not hear his question, but I heard her answer in the tone that mothers use when they are speaking a truth to be passed on: "You can't have a war without people being killed."

Yes, mother: "You can't have a war without people being killed."

Yes, child: "You can't have a war without people being killed."

That is a truth as old as any you can name from any ancient Greek whose name is hard to spell. We have always known it, but we still build war monuments to it.

Maybe someday we will be able to judge the arrival of peace when we build a monument for the living and the words etched on its highly reflective surface would be:

We won't have a war, so people can live.

And that monument will be totally above the ground so it will never disappear.

El Salvador

The first spanking
I ever got was for
something I have
long, long forgotten.
But it had something
to do with who I
have become.

Some carry their
dreams in their
pockets and after
years of rubbing
they become too
worn even to put
in a scrapbook.

Mothers sleep twice
at night:
once in their children
and
once in themselves.

When
you
walk
the
dog
have
you
ever
tried
to
walk
in
front
of
it
?

How cruel peace would be
to those who live to
devour others.

A songbird knows
one song and makes
of it a life worth
living.

Peace hides until
you get the nerve
to shout out loud:
"I will do it!"

There are no
rainbows at
night because
people don't
look.

There are windows that
will not open. If I
use a brick, where
can I keep the
pieces of glass
if I change my
mind?

Children tell the truth
until they are old enough
to realize they can some-
times get what they want
by not telling the truth.
At that age they become
adults.

The microwave oven is
the wrong invention for
the support of peacemaking.

It has buttons to press
and time to reduce.

Holding hands while
waiting for the kettle
to whistle is much
better.

I run so far God
is waiting for me.

To sit on a porch
as the day ends,
to think of satisfaction
    and the need of a better
    dream tomorrow.

Nicaragua

From Enemies to Friends

One way to understand the 1989 events in Europe that led to the tearing down of the Berlin Wall was expressed by a Czechoslovakian pastor, Milan Opocensky. He said it was a longing for wholeness, to be able to live in truth, and to have the same in your heart as on your lips. Perhaps the wall came down because Germans decided to make their world whole, to unite in truth instead of remaining divided by untruth.

When I was growing up in the 1940s, Germany was an enemy. We won the war against them but then split them into two. The West one became a friend, and we helped them rebuild after the war. The East one became an enemy, and they built a wall to separate themselves from us.

Then, out of the blue, the wall came down in November 1989 and within months the two Germanys were working out a way to reunite. Suddenly it was as if the past no longer mattered; it was the future that counted.

Enemies are not always real. If we say they are, then they are. But if we say they are not, they are not. It turns out that it is mostly a matter of convenience. We can change from enemies to friends. We just have to take the wall down, whether of stone or of thought.

How can we talk of love and curse enemies? What is the fear in our hearts that creates enemies?

Childhood Fiction Turned Truth

At the top of the stairs of my childhood was a doorway marked Forever. I could see it clearly in the summer months when time stretched to standing still between school grades. Between getting out of one grade and starting another there was always enough time to do everything and to be bored by nothing to do.

I suspect my mother knew the doorway was there too, and it was care that made her call me in after dark on days when I rode my bike so much my feet would keep pedaling hours after I was in bed. (Though I don't ride a bike as an adult, I carry still the habit of churning in bed at night.)

Her duty was what was expected of a good mother, but I know also now that it was born of the fear that I might one night remember those stairs and make a mad dash for the door. Gone. And it would be forever for her too. Mothers believe in what their children know, and their agony is to watch it be replaced by the lies of the world, by those who say the lies over and over until they believe them and thereby convince themselves they had never seen such a doorway.

Truth is that which replaces what they know. So defined, life becomes duty, not fascination. Life becomes death trapped in duty. Life lived in denial of staircases with doorways waiting at the top.

Life without staircases because it is too much trouble to climb.

United States

Sand castles in the air
can be built from dreams

and skate keys and a half
dozen other pocket secrets

of an eight-year-old.

And they'll last there
until an adult comes

along who is too busy to
look for a lost shoe and

turns the castle into a
footprint.

So many of the windows
are stuck. I think of
rocks to throw at them
but remember that some
days it rains.

What changes is the future;
What stays the same is the
present;
No one remembers the past
correctly.

A smile on the face of

A child with a hunger-bloated
belly is

A choice of which one to look
at and which one to do
something about.

I don't see truth
every day,

nor rainbows,

but

I believe in both.

A child, hungry,

does not have arms

long enough to

reach my plate.

balloons have limits.
each one, never mind
its color or shape,
will only get so big
and then:
blam!

the wizard in each of us
needs nourishment so
wonder will be loosed
again in the world

Tricycles are for playing,
not to go places.

Maybe our world would
improve if adults had
tricycles . . .

and
shyer smiles.

Guatemala

New Messages for the Living

(Dry Tears for Dry Bones)

For the second time in my life I was in Leningrad. For the second time I was confronted with trying to understand the clash of 900 days of a wartime siege between the spirit and will of the Germans and the spirit and will of the Russians. Once again, in that presence, my soul was made quiet as granite waiting for a sculptor to discover it and give it some life.

With the odds so much in the Germans' favor in 1942 how could they not take the city? By the end of those 900 days the people of Leningrad had been reduced to surviving on one-half slice of bread per person to divide into three meals for a day.

What pride of the Leningrad people was placed in opposition to the military zeal of the Germans? Did the Germans fail because, after all, they were human and knew, deep inside, that they were up against a spirit that was more than human?

For the second time in my life I visited the memorial cemetery in Leningrad where the 700,000 who died in the 900-day siege were buried in mounds of 10,000 graves. The day was gray. March. Soviet March, still winter. Some wind, cold. The flowers laid on the grave markers were a contrast to the drabness of winter not yet left. The nearby lake was still iced over.

Some had placed candy on the markers, and some a cube of sugar. All I could think of was to leave a coin as a wish for never again, as a memory of my having been there, a memory I would also take with me.

It is not my habit to visit cemeteries, but if I lived in Leningrad I would go often to that cemetery at times when the tour buses and the masses they bring would not be there. I would go at all seasons and make a connection through change to the unchanging of the tragic history that brought their deaths.

As I walked alone past mound after mound of the ten thousands, I had dry tears for dry bones. Why don't we visit cemeteries to meet again the dead in order to find new messages for the living?

Haiti

Songs of the glory time:
singing loud is more
important than on key.

Walking straight lines
in a dense forest means
short walks.

walking on a summer sidewalk
with eyes closed guessing at
where the cracks are

I wore copper shoes.
Got up an hour early
every morning to polish
them and learned to
walk so they wouldn't
scuff. My favorite
part was when kids
would stop me so they
could see their
reflections in the
shiny copper.

the colors of . . .

—Parker ink spilled in the ocean

—grass for lying on at the
height of spring

—blush, of a first serious
surprised kiss

—whining of a thirsty puppy

—the stare of an eagle, and

—morning glow the first day
after you've been sick for
a week

hunger and anger are
the inside out of
each other

The collection of flowers
in my hand wilted even
though I held them high
to show them the water
in the pond.

Walking by a white picket
fence with my fingers out,
silently raking a stick
along the pickets and
hearing the clacking of
my childhood. Should I
run and make it faster,
louder?

green grass stains on my heart from
wrestling with memories of those days
of summertime eternity when I would
wait until dark to come in so my
mother would not see the grass stains
on my pants from the heroic abandonment
of everything I tried was possible.

at eighty,
frail because of no work
left in a body covered
by the wind tracks of time,
heavy on a soul destined
to be the salt of the earth,
trodden into the compost of
history as one of the
tasteless masses that make
riches possible

for
others.

Guatemala

Myself in the Stranger

The White Castle eatery is an American institution that cuts across a lot of cultural segments. The small smothered-in-onions hamburgers are sold like hotcakes to a wide variety of people: construction workers, police, office workers, retired folks, truck drivers, men and women in business suits, old and young alike.

One day I went to a White Castle to be alone with my concerns, to have a lunch where I would not be bothered. But as it happened I was adopted by a black gentleman of seventy or more. He was in front of me in line. He walked very slowly and stammered when he talked. But he was warmhearted, quick to smile, and outgoing. He told the clerk taking orders that he wanted a Pepsi and french fries. She asked him if he wanted anything else and with some difficulty he stammered that he would like "what that lady had." He was referring to another worker behind the counter and so the clerk said, "Hamburgers?" Thinking slowly as if to recognize that word for the first time, he finally said, "Yes."

She asked how many but by now he was visibly confused and didn't answer. To help him she prompted, "Three?" "Yes, yes, yes," he replied. When they came to his tray along with his Pepsi and fries, he exclaimed, "Three! Three? Oh, well, I guess I said three."

When I got my order and began to look for a table I saw that he had been standing and waiting for me to find a table together. We found one and he began to talk. He saw that I had ketchup and he didn't, so I gave him one of mine. But he could not get it open, and after I opened it for him he thanked me with a warmth that startled me in its genuineness.

He asked me what kind of car I drove. "Toyota," I said. "Oh," he replied, "I drive a Ford. LTD." Then he told me he was a widower and his wife had died about eight years ago. God had called her home but when his time would come to be called—well, then they would be together again.

After a pause to stare, he chuckled and said that sometimes he gets into mischief. But he quickly added that he didn't touch the women. I offered the thought that as long as he didn't get into trouble, maybe mischief was OK. He didn't answer, his eyes focusing into the distance of wherever he was at that moment—in the past or in the future. I had no way of knowing.

I had gone to the White Castle for a lonely lunch and was adopted by an elderly stranger. Our lives were so different, and yet it seemed clear that we had been put together for ten minutes for a purpose. Was the time mainly for him or for me?

Our conversation was of no consequence, yet it had an importance for me beyond the words. Ten minutes of my life on a day when I wanted to be alone and a stranger gently forced his way into my awareness.

Why a stranger? I left wondering why we are taught to fear strangers, to sometimes make of them enemies and people we have to control. We do not have to take justice into account when the other person is unknown.

How can I find myself in the stranger? And thereby begin to be taught love, not fear?

Nicaragua

God's patience is to wait
in the eyes of poor
children,
patience also to wait
for us to look into them.

If the paint were to
peel off the hungry children,
would we do more about them?

The stars really
are holes in the
sky. The problem
is they are too
far away for us
to look through,
but maybe not
for those on
the other side.

God never rests.
The moon is blue once
in a blue moon.

My mother told me one;
the other I figured
out for myself.

Fourth-grade girls who meet
quiet at camp and learn names
the first time around and
after a week believe that
when they part they will
write forever and the world
will wait for them to grow
up as goodbyes are shared of
fervent promises and no
knowledge yet of the loss
of memories.

I am so good,
so good running before
the wind.

I am so good God tires of
waiting and I worship with
empty heart,
waiting. . . .

Yes, Mom, I remember to keep my
feet dry. But I think you forgot
to tell those who spill blood on
our feet, never looking down.

Outside my window is a
rose that changes color
each day.

I wonder why God didn't
think of that?

Dreams are someone else's
memories momentarily lost.

That is why it is good
to share them.

Ecuador

A Messenger from God

God can appear suddenly and silently. At least, God's messengers can. I was sitting with my wife on the polluted shore of the Hudson River at Stony Point, New York. My attention had been mostly on some ducks swimming off a small jutting of rocks to our left. I looked away, and when I turned back toward the ducks I was startled to see an elderly woman picking her way along the bank. I was also astonished to wonder how she had made her way through the branches of a tree that were hanging down to the water's edge.

The woman came our way and stopped in front of us to declare, "Isn't this terrible?" We guessed she was referring to the pollution of various kinds of junk along the shoreline. Not waiting for a reply from us she launched into a long rambling lament, as much directed to us as to anyone who would care to listen. Her lament was about a dead dog left on the beach for fourteen months and a dead deer left near the sidewalk for weeks. Then it was about the war we might get into (an unstated but understood reference to the Middle East).

We began to chat a bit, the kind of chatter of strangers. For her side we learned that she had come to the United States as an immigrant from Europe at eighteen when one had to pass tests of health and of having some money. "Not at all like today," she said, "when we have millions who are illegal, into drugs and who knows what."

Then, suddenly, she got to the punch line: "Why can't we have elected officials who look out for the common good?" I was awestruck and felt as if I had been turned to stone, for I knew then that this woman was more than a woman, she was a messenger of God. She had started with the lament of people not caring and so dead animals were left around even though she had called the officials about it. Then, without changing tone or expression, she dropped the message of who on earth is looking out for the common good?

Was this woman a messenger God had made up just minutes before, created out of that which God has for creation? Or was this messenger a woman that God had laid a hand on and said, "You are now seventy-nine years old but I have a message for you to leave. And so as you walk around talking to those who will listen and to those who won't, this is what I want you to say: 'Who is looking out for the common good?'"

In a different fashion I felt the question from God as "What are you doing with my creation?" We were sitting in the presence of human-made pollution, a flotsam of cans, paper, plastic, and discarded appliances of convenience (but also obsolescence) lining the riverbank. Yet we were equally sitting in the presence of human-made arrogance: the decision of men (men, not women) to go to war with Iraq, to cause a few hundred thousand deaths, and to do unprecedented environmental damage—all as the "only prudent decision" that could be made.

Standing before us was a woman who had come to the United States as an eighteen-year-old ready and willing to work, "not for money," she said, "we had so little of that, but for the good." Now at seventy-nine she was taking afternoon walks along a polluted shoreline, saying to anyone or no one that the only thing she has to look forward to is war and despair. That was the painful result of her sixty-one years of labor as an immigrant to the promised land. The promise, in the end, had been a bad one.

She said a gracious goodbye and shuffled off. I didn't follow her leaving, not wanting to know God's secret: Would she just disappear or continue on as a woman? She had been a messenger and that was enough.

Who is looking out for the common good?

Guatemala

To walk on the wind
is done better with
hands waving like
it was a tightrope.

Is there a kid
inside you?
Or have you
outgrown the
need for growth?

the wonder of it all is
how love first happens
when a moment before
it had not

songs that have
no words or tunes
drown out all the
others in my mind

Doughnuts are round
so they can have
holes in them.

I carry an open umbrella,
even on dry, cold days.
Hiding from God is easy
if you just pretend that
you don't notice anyone
looking.

I wear a red carnation
in my lapel when I get
off planes to see who
might meet me.

Gypsies tell the truth
but they never stay in
the same place.

That is why truth
changes.

Counting to ten with
colors.

Can you?

The memories of my mother
before I was born. I have
to be very still, very still
to find them.

Songs I sing when I want to
sing of something else.

Throwing rocks through open
windows unless it is raining.

Truth always wears
a disguise. It is
when you see through
it that the moment
comes.

Nicaragua

Jesus on Our Doorstep

I was on the veranda of the Pax Guest House on Mount Saint Benedict, overlooking Tunapuna, a small community near the airport in Trinidad. The morning was cool. Some rain clouds were visible, but as they were quite high it seemed they would blow over without delivering rain.

My mood was one of deep perplexity. For three days I had been attending a consultation with church friends from Jamaica, Guyana, Trinidad, Grenada, the United States, and Canada. Bill Watty, Caribbean Methodist Pastor Theologian, had given the opening address on the topic "Jesus on Our Doorstep." It would not let go of me, nor would I let go.

Bill had had a lot to say that day about Jesus and the church. He suggested that Emperor Constantine had pulled off the greatest coup in history by legitimatizing the church. He brought it in from the doorstep of society and made it the guest of honor. As Bill put it, "The storm of persecution subsided, the fires were quenched, the sword was returned to its sheath, the lions were returned to their cages and the despised sect was elevated to the status of the State Religion."

The problem was that the agenda of the church shifted to being an alibi for the world's "business as usual." Though the church stayed "inside," Jesus returned to the doorstep to be among those whom both the world and the church had forgotten. In our time, Bill posited, the blessing of Liberation Theology is that it blows the cover, calls the bluff, and exposes the church as privilege.

The question for the church is not a "preferential option for the poor." The church does not have an option. It was not Bill's purpose to turn against the church. The actions of his life show the deepest passion for the church. The question he was posing to the church was what was it going to do with Jesus on its doorstep?

Should the church bring Jesus in and make him one of us, like us? Or could it be that Jesus stands on the doorstep saying that our house has become desolate and he is here to ask us to come out? Could it be that Jesus is asking us to follow him into the wilderness, to go to him outside the gate (Hebrews 13:12–14)? Could it be that Jesus is saying that if we continue as we are, we are doomed?

I don't know, Bill. And that is what troubles me. . . .

Guatemala

I went around the house
and took all the glass
out of the windows. Then

I put each glass back in a
different window because

I had grown tired of seeing
the same thing over and
over out my windows.

A bird sings a sweet song on
a tree. I don't know the name
of either, nor of the child I
saw in the street hungry. . . .

Shadows under clouds are
never free of the wind.

Love is also obedient
when it is freely given.

Would you be surprised
to learn the moon is
really a round window?

It does no good to count
the stars. Someone
always asks me why I am
standing so still . . . and
I lose the count.

I went to bed with
my all-day sucker
still in my mouth.

I never was in a
hurry with grape
flavor.

A row of corn
so straight
so long
the farmer dreamed
of feeding the
world from it.

God don't give no transfers:
every day has its own fare,
can't ride on the one gone by.

Those who know they are
right never look at the
stars. Why bother to
count if there would be
one more, or less?

Where is your twin?

In a forest of seedlings
there is no one with
memory that is still to
come.

Those with memory will
be the ones who cut
the forest down.

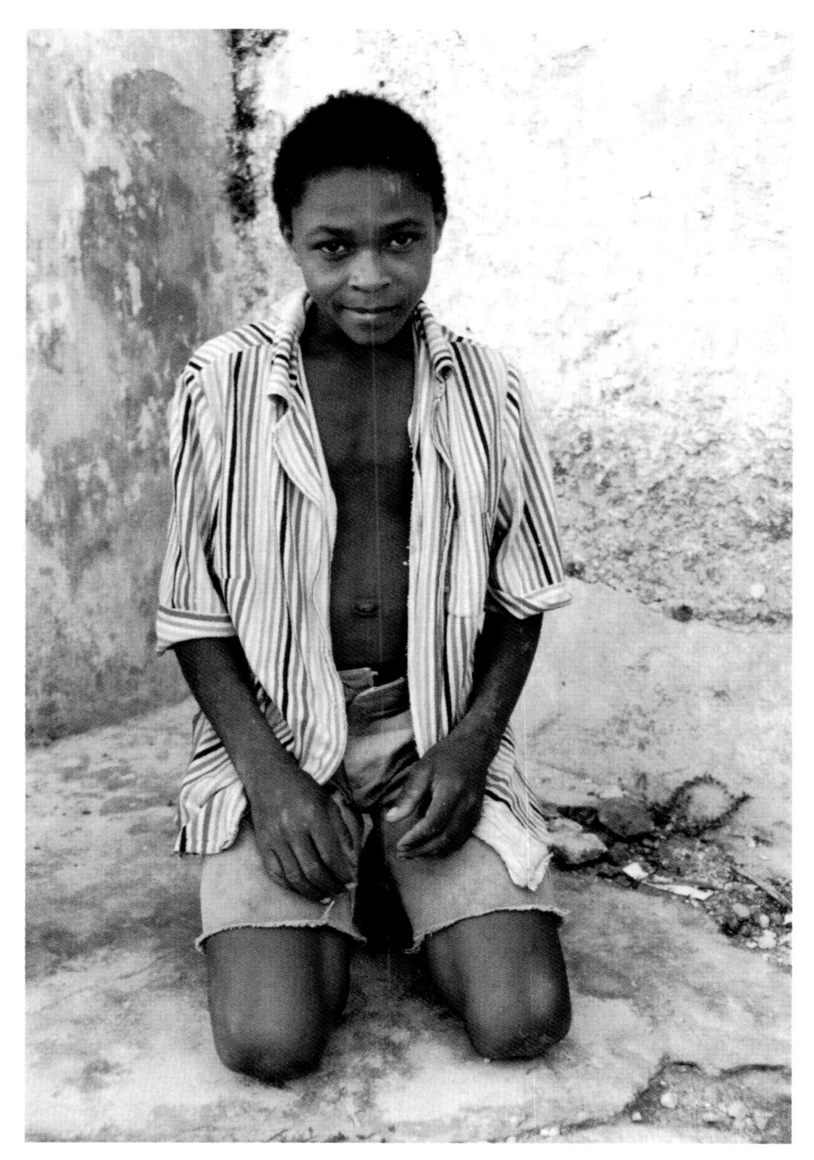

Haiti

Does God Exist?

When I was a small boy my brother Jerry, five years older, convinced me that God had elves, fairies, angels, whatever you want to call them, that were assigned to me and every other person to follow them around and see how they behaved. This was especially important for children around Christmastime, as somehow these "followers" got their message to Santa Claus also. He didn't explain this, and I was afraid to ask. Being connected to God was worry enough; I didn't want to complicate matters by getting into the Santa Claus part.

And so it was that I would practice running around corners in my house to get fast enough to be able to catch one of the elves or whatevers being just a bit slow one time, so I would see one . . . and thereby prove the existence of God. A big task for a small boy, but I was determined and not even deterred by the many times I had to make excuses for dashing around a corner only to run into my mother or father coming the other way.

As an adult I have realized that God cannot be approached from the point of view of proof. My Western scientific worldview is sufficient for living in the world but not for matters of involvement with meaning in the world. God's involvement in my life (and others) is not something physical like an elf assigned to monitor behavior. God comes to me (and others) in another way. I am a receiver and face always the choice of interacting or not.

The essence of what my brother was confronting me with as a small boy was not that of being spied upon but was I doing right?

Sidewalks and Porches

I live now in a neighborhood where people walk. The sidewalks are a direction for travel that allow conversation, not cussing at the stupidity of another driver. A neighbor just passed and we talked awhile in Spanish. He is French but lived near the border of Spain and grew up speaking both. He speaks Spanish better than the English he has learned in seven years here. I would have never known any of this going around in a car. Sidewalks slow you down to talk.

We never had a porch swing when I was a boy. But I remember summer nights when Mom and Dad would fill our small front porch with their sitting while my brother and I played anywhere we wanted as long as they could see us. Dusk meant coming closer, which we didn't like, for it meant being close enough to be called in for a bath and bed to end what until then had been a never-ending day.

People would sit outside, but the porches on our street were not the kind in the city on the old houses: two-storied, close together, large full front porches with high ceilings and sometimes even a wooden railing waist high.

Now I'm over fifty and have a porch and a white swing and a neighborhood where people walk. I see again all my playmates and boyhood neighbors, though I haven't figured out yet which one can be Dell, who lived next door. She was a lot shorter than those who walk by now. I often wondered what adults who didn't grow up past kid size thought about that, and I never had the nerve to ask Dell. Lately it's things like that that I am trying to figure out while swinging on my porch between my childhood, when I didn't have one, and now, when I do.

Cuba

corners
can
be made
round if
you go
around
them
slowly
enough

too many who search
for peace get so
wrapped up in their
way they forget to
leave clear footsteps
for others to follow

I have no energy;
blow me up, God,

like a balloon
and let me go. . . .

to lie on the beach
is dangerous, not
from the sun . . . but
if you are willing
to let go of all
those sounds of
busyness and
importance inside
to have the
ancient, unceasing
sound of the
ocean surf take
over, the next
sound could well
be God

I had a pencil once that
I thought would last
forever, and then one day
I didn’t need to use it
and when I thought to
look—it was gone.
One day is all it takes
to make a forever.

Life is not a photo album
but we live it like curling
papers in a shoe box high
on a closet shelf waiting
to be found and remembered
by God.

I sneak into a chapel
pretending God does not
notice. The more I close
my eyes the more God sees.
I can't decide if I am
there to empty or be
filled. Neither one wins
so I sneak out.

I
Think
I
Saw
A
Blue
Cloud.

Hold up your hand if
you saw it too.

kites flying children

counting leaves until
I had a tree

candles lit in the
wind take more
matches

Nicaragua

Wholesight

(One-eyed Living)

Parker J. Palmer opens his book *To Know As We Are Known: A Spirituality of Education* with the provocative image, "Many of us live one-eyed lives." The thesis he develops stems from the metaphor that we have two eyes. One is the eye of the mind, which we use to form our image of reality, and the other is the eye of the heart, which looks "for realities to which the mind's eye is blind." Our task is to develop a vision of the world in which we use both eyes. We need "wholesight," which unites mind and heart.

For Palmer it is not enough to know, we must also seek the relationships that exist with that knowing. This means, for him, the linking of knowledge with compassion, for it is a key linkage that has been pushed aside by our demand for objective mind's-eye knowledge.

This also means we must learn to regain our spiritual heritage and seek knowledge that originates in compassion or love. We must find new ways to see with our heart and combine them with the ways in which we see with our mind. The important relationship to be rediscovered is that "a knowledge born of compassion aims not at exploiting and manipulating creation but at reconciling the world to itself."

Is that kind of knowledge possible for us? In a scientific age the premium is on knowledge that is factual and unchanging. Our time wants knowledge that can be used, and therefore it must be reliable and controllable.

Dare we take seriously the relationship of something like compassion or love to knowledge? Won't that introduce emotion and unreliability to knowing, make it something that changes rather than staying the same so we can count on it? How can we be sure if love is involved in what we know?

Instead of answering questions put that way, first think about what we want knowledge for. What do we want to know so that the world we live in can be a better one? Parker's answer is that if we want a knowledge that will heal our broken world, we will have to change the kind of knowledge we rely on now.

If we are going to think seriously about the impossible, about coloring the wind, about changing the world, we are going to have to be serious about compassion and love. Without their connection to what we know, our knowledge is incomplete—and dangerous.

Russia

Magic I have believed in since
I was a boy and
I first saw it rain gently.

gray woodsmoke closed
my eyes
involuntarily
and I was glad
to disguise
the tears I had
been carrying as
extra weight
in the present
that had
forked from the
past I thought
had a chance
to be future

the
doggedness of change
has sandwiched
my actions between
between
being sorry
and
scared

I
hold a match
I'm
afraid to
light

and so kids don't walk to
school anymore or learn to
count from fence posts or
rocks that can make it all
the way by foot to school

the two countries that have a war
with the generals having it out
everyone else cheering will have
invented something to carry all
of us farther than the wheel

fall's purpose is the new life

the mountains know well how
to care for distances

I slept with the tension of
an iron skillet

I don't remember my
childhood depending on green
jelly beans, but I guess maybe
it did

Have you ever swung so high
in a swing that you stopped
at the very top and wondered
if you held your breath
would you stay there forever?

Running through childhood is
best done slowly for as the
years add up so do other things
that will slow down the
running anyway.

Walking between rain puddles
until I get curious enough
about what is around me and
look up and accept wet feet
as the price.

and the days run
away like horses
over the hill

new wineskins
old thoughts
and the patience
to wait

Cuba

Take Time to Go Out Through the Kitchen

The quite small lady was in a white nun's outfit, trimmed a lightish blue, and she was bundled over with a heavy cardigan sweater, industrial-grade black. She came into the packed ballroom with head bowed as if she were only half size. When she mounted the podium to speak her first movement was a bow, hands folded before her in greeting and submission. Her manner was clearly to shrink so much in human size that what was left was God's word spoken larger than life.

Mother Teresa was until then a media name to me. Someone I admired. Though her views on abortion were different from mine, it was clear from the first moment of her presence in the room that that was not the impact inside me. Only hours later was I able to glimpse what had quieted me as I listened to her speak.

Her words were so fresh. It was as if I had heard the actual words of Jesus. The two thousand years of distance had disappeared. It was as if Mother Teresa had talked with Jesus that morning and was repeating his words that afternoon. I was hearing the gospel only one person removed from Jesus, not from two thousand years of being passed on.

What made me understand was learning those hours later that when she left the packed auditorium, absorbing an avalanche of dozens of flash photos, she asked to be taken through the kitchen on her way out of the hotel. When she got there she stopped to talk with the workers. I suppose that only Jesus and Mother Teresa would have thought of that. The least ones, always on their minds and in their actions.

Living the Dream

What dream?

In the conversation between Alice and the Cheshire Cat in *Alice in Wonderland* she asked which way she should go from where she was. The Cat's answer was, "That depends a good deal on where you want to get to."

Yes, what dream?

Alice's reply was that she didn't much care, to which the Cat answered, "Then it doesn't matter which way you go."

Yes, what dream?

"Just as long as I get *somewhere,*" said Alice.

But where is *your* somewhere? What is the dream you are living?

Let me see what colors you put on the wind. . . .

Russia

I wanted to have a dream
where I was sure of myself,
caught every ball,
and spelled every word
like the big unopened
dictionary in the hall.

And to collect old bottle
caps in memory of days of
my grandfather and grand-
mother, when porches and
running boards were places
for kids.

And when everything was
o.k. because it was all
I knew.

windows have to be
clean on both sides
to do any good

no hurry;
I need rest before
I catch up

rest from
my abundance

Running water is an easy image,

running flowers is not. We're

used to colors standing still.

I wind colors into
a huge ball, which
I carry deep in my
winter coat pocket
for those moments
when
I need to remember.

Mommy,
Where would you
hide a rain?

Cuba

Once stripes choose a direction
the rest is easy.

When we're grown up a whole
bunch of things get labeled
impossible and though I can't
explain how a telephone works
I know it does and never mind.

It is a matter of choosing
direction—
of not worrying that the
channel
does not exist but
worrying
that it does.

at 94,
or 7,

the dreams are really
the same:

only
the age differs

Cuba